MAKING LEARNING FUN

Marion Aldred

MINERVA PRESS
LONDON
MIAMI RIO DE JANEIRO DELHI

MAKING LEARNING FUN
Copyright © Marion Aldred 2000

All Rights Reserved

ISBN 0 75411 366 3

First Published 2000 by
MINERVA PRESS
315–317 Regent Street
London W1R 7YB

Printed in Great Britain for Minerva Press

MAKING LEARNING FUN

The Introduction

My purpose writing this book is to encourage and motivate my daughter – and hopefully other children also – to learn, and to keep her interested in wanting to learn about everything around her.

As you turn the pages, you will read about everyday awareness and situations that children will come up against, and how they will need to have a flexible approach around others, and be able to handle themselves.

This book helps support and guide your child or children with self-confidence and building their self-esteem, in everyday communications in conversation, recognising and demonstrating understanding of their needs, showing a caring response to questions and how they can be answered.

The theme is always 'making learning fun'. The key factor is being able to demonstrate and give examples of everyday surroundings from my own experience as an adult, of why I responded in a particular way, and what the result was.

The most important factor to realise is that learning is not a competition. You do not always have to get everything right. It is okay to get things wrong, because this is how we learn to put things right.

The Opening Thought

In the beginning on 19 May, 1993, I gave birth to a baby girl called Carla Marie Duval. This is the day she was born. This is why it is called her birthday, and this is how my thoughts on writing *Making Learning Fun* came about.

In everyday conversations I was continuously realising that it was not what I said to my daughter, Carla, or how I said something, but it was always being able to give a clear explanation of why I responded in a particular way. It didn't make a difference if it was to do with good behaviour, or a sudden, bad, frustrating mood, or if it was really to do with my not feeling in a good mood at that particular moment, and the day itself having been full of negative, disappointing encounters which caused me to feel resentful and hostile in my approach towards everything and everyone.

The changearound came when I realised that my method of approach was not very beneficial for my present relationship with my daughter or for her later on when she became an adult. She would start to withdraw, feel uncomfortable and this could cause uncertainties of feelings which could lead to difficulties in sociability and progression at school. Improvement was necessary.

To get on better with my daughter I looked on the inside, and communicated more openly, honestly and directly about whatever the matter was on the surface, and I also listened to myself more carefully in how I talked with Carla. The result in our relationship was that we now get on better by responding to each other in a more caring way in freely open communication. If something was wrong, I was confident that Carla would feel reassured, loved, cared for and supported enough to talk openly and tell me about it. I would always show understanding and take time out in any way I could to help.

Mummy, Why Do You Write?

The birth of my self-expression as a writer started, Carla, when a tear dropped from my eyelid onto a piece of paper set before me on a wooden table. My tears completely drenched the paper with big heavy blotches, giving out a description of the despair within my eyes. My appearance resembled rainfall images pouring down continuously, heavily, beating on the paper. In anxious confusion, in all doubt and no hope, I picked up the nearby pen and started to write. Questions. Questions in my mind. How did I feel? What was making me so sad? How did I get into this uncomfortable situation? What was I going to do now?

Focusing on every detail of a word, a comment, a phrase, an expression or sound set before me, I would visualise the moment immaculately, prolong it into a chapter, and conclude with an episode of my life. My thoughts, my fears, my suggestions. A sudden awakening. Whether a new idea or an ending. An adventure, a mystery, my individual opinion on whatever my mind would approach on appeal.

Every hour, every minute, every second is so precious. In which respect? To live each day as if it's your last and to reflect on the moment. I did the best I could, resulting in having feelings of contentment rather than regret. In my experience, I can acknowledge what happened yesterday. I cannot see what tomorrow will bring. I only have fruitful thoughts of images and visions of hopeful ideas and well-being.

The Approach Towards Learning

The approach towards learning is important, and that is to carefully listen and concentrate on what is being taught to you. This makes things easier to remember.

At times you might feel put off by feelings of boredom, restlessness, feeling a little weary and disinterest. Helpful suggestions are to try having regular breaks, taking time out to do something else, or just have a rest for a while. Then hopefully you will be able to feel more relaxed and refreshed and ready to start again.

Learning is not a competition. It should be about enjoying what you are being taught, and seeing how you can make the most of this, realising, as you learn more, that you can gain and benefit from what you have achieved when you are an adult your choice of pathway. My daughter, Carla, says to me, 'Mummy, I would like to be a teacher when I am grown up.'

Always ask questions to find out about things you do not know. Never be withdrawn or shy and think, This has been explained to me more than once, and I am going to look silly and feel embarrassed if I ask again.

No, you are never silly when you are wanting to learn; it is when you stop learning by not asking questions that difficulties occur. Keep trying when you find something difficult, and this will make things easier to learn, giving you confidence and reassurance to carry on trying.

Listening and Learning from the Teacher
At Home and At School

Your first teacher is usually the one who gave birth to you. This person is your mother.

From the beginning in the home environment we are taught right and wrong, and what the differences are in our behaviour, and what type of reaction we would get depending on whether our behaviour is right or wrong.

Even as a baby, before sounds or words or sentences come out of our mouth, we are taught instructions of discipline from our first teacher's actions which speak louder than words. As we reach an age where we are able to talk and have a conversation and give our opinions on what we like and also what we don't like, we are more aware of our surroundings. This is called education. Education is all about learning. Making learning fun is very important so that you are interested in learning about different things at home and at school. As you become an adult, having an education behind you helps you to find out more about yourself and make choices about what you want to do when you are grown up. Education is also the way to all the nice things you do when you are an adult and have fun.

'Mummy, do I have to have an education?'

'No, Carla, you do not have to have an education.'

But having education behind you does help you to feel more confident about yourself and the decisions you will need to make when you are an adult.

Being able to read and write is all to do with the entrance on the topic of English. Reading is very important. It is useful for learning about why we do certain things and also why we do not. Reading explains many subjects, and gives many examples of questions, and can also help with answering them for you. Also reading can keep you interested in wanting to learn about other countries and places and explain their way of life.

Writing is equally as important, because, as you get older, your signature and your personal details are things about yourself which are always asked for, and quite often, if you cannot respond by writing this information down, you can miss out by not having permission to do something you would like to do. Also there is no proof of your existence in the world of a record cannot be found about you. After you are born, your parents have six weeks to register you at the registry office at their local town hall. This is a place where you are first recognised as existing in the world, and where all your personal details are written down, and both parents' signatures are required. Another example is if there is a sudden emergency at home you can help by giving your personal details to the police or ambulance person.

Going up the stairs is how I will introduce maths and its various important uses, continuously adding numbers onto one another until you reach the top for the answer. Going down the stairs is how I will describe subtraction of numbers, taking one number from another, and finally when you reach the bottom of the stairs there are no stairs to subtract. Zero take away zero equals zero.

Every day we are surrounded by maths and its useful multiple purposes in many different ways. For example, every year you have a birthday. This year you were five years old. Next year you will be six years old. Five plus one equals six. Another example is: five fingers take away four fingers equals one finger. Five minus four equals one. The message of maths in this chapter is count in values, always thinking about what you can add up and achieve in life.

Patience

The more you understand about things the clearer things will become. Never feel that you are expected to know everything by a certain age to do with life's experiences of ups and downs.

To be calm and patient means to think first about why you should do something or why you should not do something, especially if it has been explained to you first of all.

Be proud of yourself for who you are on the inside, and let it shine on the outside, for what you have achieved from your efforts, determination, consistent trying and not giving up. A little patience every day can go a long, long way.

Try to take each day as it comes, enjoying the basic pleasures of being healthy and fit, and by taking care of your body in what you eat and how you think.

The nice things are those which feel good all round, although at times you may feel neglected and feel you don't get recognised enough for being a nice person, treating others as you would like to be treated, having good manners and a kind, caring nature.

Think back to what you learned when you were a little girl, and then growing into a teenager, then a young lady and now an adult.

Apply all this knowledge to make a happy adult life for yourself in whatever you choose to do.

Scared

To be scared means to feel uncertain, unsure or to feel unsafe around someone or something or even a group of people.

You must never be afraid. The way to approach this unsettled feeling is to be brave by always sticking up for yourself, and being strong and independent in what you say and how you say it, supported by your actions. Always be prepared for good and bad days, or even happy and sad moments.

What is most important is your approach to being able to cope and deal with unexpected situations. You can do this by accepting that this is all normal in individuals' behaviour, although it is not nice at times. The best way to deal with this is not to get upset, but be able to see it as a learning experience.

Money

The outward pleasure of having a lot of money is being able to do what you want, and how you want it, or alternatively being able to pay someone to do something you would like done, and having the choice of not having to do it yourself. Can you have too much money at times? Having money put aside teaches you patience and discipline regarding handling money and also to have values. Looking on the inside, can it bring summer, sunshine, smiles, or does it bring waterfalls of tears, resembling only shadows of a portrait reflecting continuous sadness or discontent.

It's not the amount of money you have at times, it is what you do with it to bring about a sense of achievement and purpose from it, hopefully giving you a happier feeling on which to feed and prosper.

When you are working, try and put some of your money in the bank, your post office book, or the building society, so that if you want to buy something that is quite expensive you can turn to your savings, which is money you have put aside until it is needed. Having faith, hope and a thought for tomorrow or the near future can help, so if you sensibly put a little money aside you are in a position to be able to make a difference and do something about it, and hopefully feel pleased at the outcome, rather than having negative thoughts, such as, What's the point of saving when there are so many things I would like now? I may not even live to see tomorrow. It's true that anything can happen to you at any moment, but let's think positive – you never know what lies around the corner.

Wrong Behaviour

Try not to copy wrong behaviour because you feel that when you do the right thing no one notices you. Try to question and notice yourself on the inside first. Consider why you react in a particular way and respond on the outside. Is it for the better, or for unfair treatment from a circumstance or a situation, or even a barrier of protection for yourself, with inner personal thoughts like, No one will really know what I am about, I am in my shell of armour, it's my daily dress code of uniform.

You are your mirror's reflection, always reflecting back to yourself, should I have or should I have not? Be true to yourself on the inside in a positive way and on the outside too.

We all behave badly at times, adults as well as children. It is quite normal to behave badly sometimes, but constant wrong behaviour is not good and you might be punished, which means you will miss out on something nice because of your wrong behaviour.

Why spend your time misbehaving, when there is nothing you can learn from this? If you are upset about something and this is why you behave in a wrong way, for someone to notice you, this is not good. Try talking to someone you trust, who will listen to you carefully and hopefully help you to feel better about yourself, and also help you to change your mind about wrong behaviour and see more value in receiving compliments and behaving in a more pleasant way, now that your behaviour is good, from the inside, and on the outside to.

Good Behaviour

That which is good is often not noticed, and you feel put off at times, thinking, This lack of attention towards me and my hard efforts is unjustified. You must not be upset by this, because God notices everything and he will reward you unexpectedly.

You must always try and encourage and motivate yourself in whatever you choose to do or become, although it is nice to hear a compliment and hear kind words of encouragement and support so you don't give up, you are doing well. You must not depend on the kind words of individuals to praise you for your achievements and to feel satisfied about something you have achieved. Individuals can let you down at times in their support, just when you feel like you need it most, with their lack of care. Also they are not always honest about something you have done well, when you feel proud in yourself and would like to share the feeling. Sometimes individuals can be for you, but sometimes they can be against you.

Always try to use your own judgement on how you can improve yourself but always listen to others, because it is good to share opinions on different things, so you can broaden your horizons on various subjects and learn things from each other.

Physical Appearance

How you look on the surface may enhance your self-confidence so that you feel better about yourself on the outside, but it will not make you a nice person to be around on the inside, only pleasing to the eye of an individual observer, or maybe to even more than one person.

Treating others as you would like to be treated with respect, honesty, a kind, caring, supportive, thoughtful manner to individual needs are recognised characteristics of an obviously nice person.

Take your time to get to know someone – that is, who they are on the inside. It does not matter if someone is thin or fat or white or black, beauty is a very individual and a personal concept, it is in the eyes of the beholder. Everyone has different choices. We are all different.

People

There is good and bad in all of us. Some of us consider people more than others. Some people can be kind and caring. Some people can be unkind in what they say, and how they express themselves in their actions also, sometimes knowingly and sometimes unknowingly, even strangers to us, suddenly and unexpectedly.

It can become annoying at times; the continuous, rude, aggravating behaviour on everyday travel to the shops, or when boarding a bus, for example.

This behaviour can come from all walks of life, regardless of age, colour, sex, religion, status. It's just individuals, they just seem to react how they want to, at any given moment or time, not giving a caring thought for anyone but themselves. Try to ignore this, however annoying it is at times and try not to get upset either.

Most important is your approach, knowing how to deal with all different types of people and realising from what they say or do what is important and what is not, or generally realising that some individuals just don't stop and think first, before they say or do anything.

Opportunities

Opportunities are good things. They can come as rewards of education from doing the best you can, and by seeing what this can lead up to, from doing the right thing, when at times you feel disturbed, and it can seem too easy to do otherwise and miss out.

Use your senses carefully; it helps to see only what you need to see, and to hear only what you need to hear. Take pride in yourself in how you present yourself when you leave your house, and also in how you communicate with other people. Think that there is a time and a place for everything, but unexpectedly for the better; you never know how an opportunity may come about.

Yes, sometimes coincidences can come about in sudden awareness on everyday travel, and this can be quite fortunate for you sometimes, not having to make too much effort to be where you are now. However, remember that when you get used to something that brings you great joy and happiness, and changes your life for a more fruitful surrounding, continue to look after yourself, because we can shine in the sky like stars in the night, and then all of a sudden the weather changes, just when we least expect it and heavy rainfall appears.

Try not to waste your time on responding to loud tones of echoes of nothing, which only distract you, and can spoil your concentration, and will only detain you from where you need to go or what you need to do at that particular moment. Only listen out for unexpected news of a possible change of something that could lead you in the right direction for a possible achievement of doing something well.

A seed generally grows as a result of how you feed it and look after it, although you do need to beware of individuals who might come along and mistreat it. Individuals are the same from the beginning, you do the best you can to encourage standards for growth of care, guidance, love and everything generally for the better, then someone or even several people can come along and influence you for the better or sometimes for the worst, and you need to be able to be strong, and be aware of only noticing possible positive encounters.

Developing Your Mind

Developing your mind is very important. You can help develop your mind by always looking at what you have got and not by what you have not got.

Learn to live and love yourself for who you are on the inside, and you will be able to view others more clearly for who they are on the inside also.

The outward attraction at times of individuals can be like a table full of flavoured and colourful party delights on which to munch and quench your thirst, but in reality, question things that always look nice, bright and dazzling. Always try tasting a little first, because it might not always taste as good as it looks. The same applies to all different backgrounds regardless of age or culture, or images of nicer clothes than you have yourself, or even individuals with more money than yourself. Constant viewing of so near and yet so far from the obvious at times can be deceptive, so try not to be deceived by outward appearance only.

We cannot always choose who we want to get along with. Flexibility in our approach is necessary in how we sound, and the words we use to get along with others, because at times a misunderstanding can suddenly come about, causing an outburst of fury and a loss of temper. We need to have at times a more tactful approach, thinking before we speak and always trying to remember to treat others as we would like to be treated – with respect – although it can be very difficult at times.

Some people communicate and express themselves in a friendly sociable way, listening interestedly, talking with you, asking questions and asking your opinions, and sharing their similar experiences with you, whilst others talk at you, which is not very nice. Sometimes they realise it and sometimes they do not. It can sound quite off-putting, and can come across, even if not intentionally, as aggressive, rude and very selfish, giving the impression to others that only their opinion counts and is of importance.

It's not what you say, it is how you say it that will be of importance in your conversation, explaining the subject or situation openly and honestly to the best of your understanding and knowledge from what you have learned or experienced. Have fun with words, rather than getting tongue tied, which means your words are having fun with you, as you do not know what to say. Carefully listen and choose how you will approach a situation, thinking first about how you will say something and which words you will choose to explain what you want to say.

Values

Values mean looking at what you have and responding in a grateful, thankful way.

Do you ever stop and think how lucky you are, having the bare essentials of being able to eat food everyday, wear warm or cool clothes of your choice depending on the weather, and being able to be kept in the warmth of a home to return to at the end of a good or bad day, keeping you sheltered and warm from freezing temperatures.

Every day we do take things for granted, which means we expect to have the things we need there all the time, when the unknown could occur unexpectedly changing our lives from dreams of yesterday.

Sometimes when an unfortunate accident occurs, causing a permanent injury such as the loss of an arm or a leg, it can seem like a volcano erupting causing a hazardous catastrophe of unsettlement to one's mind, which can take a while to adjust to in oneself and also physically for one's future lifestyle and well-being.

Always try to remember to give thanks every day for health and strength, with calming thoughts, such as: Tomorrow is another day; Although I feel low at the moment and so down, tomorrow is going to be what I make of it in my approach, a brighter, pleasant day to look forward to.

Quantity

Quantity means to have a lot of something. Looking at what you have got is important, rather than thinking that you haven't got a lot. Even if it's a small amount of something, try to still have quantities of appreciation for what you do have. It can be nice at times to have lots of friends, but it's worthwhile thinking about what makes nice friends, even if you just have one or two friends, look at the values in quantities of what you do like about their friendships; perhaps they are trustworthy individuals, friendly and fun to be around and also reliable.

Quantities of love, care and attention, how fortunate you are, it is not the same for everyone.

Quantities of being talked with, rather than being talked at, allowing you to have an opinion on a topic, inviting you to express that in a conversation.

Quantities of peace at last, at times to be left alone, reflecting on whatever subject you choose, in the surroundings of the four walls in your bedroom and giving opinions on topics you choose.

Quantities of positive thinking with thoughts like keep trying, even when you feel like giving up, and care is wearing you down a bit too much of late.

The turnaround in believing and having faith, and acting upon the belief that tomorrow is another day, full of challenges and opportunities in unexpected directions and possible new awakenings for a more prosperous day.

Friendships

We make friends by being friendly, but remembering that not everyone wants to be friendly. That is okay, we are all individuals, just go off and find someone who wants to become friends with you. Try not to withdraw into yourself, and feel like you said or did something wrong.

We get to know someone by introducing ourselves and having a conversation about similar interests, which means things we like and things we don't like, and our reasons for our opinions.

Quite often we don't always like everyone we meet, but it can be quite important at times to be able to get along with them, for team relationships with outsiders, so at least you know how to approach a situation rather than it controlling you, giving out an uncomfortable unsettled feeling of restlessness around you.

Shopping with Children

Shopping with a child or children starts even before entering into a shop or supermarket. On the door there is usually a sign which says 'Open' or 'Closed'.

Before entering the supermarket with my daughter, Carla, who is six years old, we get a small trolley to make things easier to carry our shopping around in. To take out a trolley in Tesco you need to have a one pound coin.

I give Carla a one pound coin, and show her where to put it in, so she can release the trolley which is connected to others and we can go and do our shopping. I explain to her that when we have finished our shopping we will get our one pound back when we connect the trolley back with the others.

When it comes to money I explain to Carla, 'Just say what you see on the coin. When you see the number or the writing, things will become much easier after a while in recognising money, whether it's pounds or pence.'

Carla says, 'Mummy, can I push the trolley around?'

I reply, 'Sure you can.'

As we go along pushing our shopping in the trolley, I ask Carla the prices of individual items, just so she can be familiar with money and how much things cost. We are in the bread section. Carla notices in the bakery that there is a clock that says one o'clock. She turns to me and says, 'Mummy, what's the time?' I show her my watch, and she says my watch says half past four, and then she asks me why the clock in the bakery says one o'clock.

I ask her to read the writing and she decides to run over to the clock. I call her back and mention to her that she has forgotten the trolley and it was her choice to push the trolley around, and also that I have given her the responsibility, so if she wants to move closer to where the clock is in the bakery, she will need to take the trolley with her.

The message I am trying to get across in this chapter of *Making Learning Fun* is that if you have a responsibility, you cannot just run away any time it suits you and return to it afterwards; you take the responsibility with you.

Carla returns with a slightly frowning face, taking the trolley and then reading the writing in the bakery, which says, 'The last time fresh bread was baked was one o'clock.' I turn to her and ask her if her question has been answered. She replies that she knows now. I respond and mention that this is why it is good to be able to read, because you can learn about lots of different things and also answer your own questions.

Prayers

Try to find time to pray, not only at times of need, or when it seems like there is no one else who cares, and the feeling is low and disappointing, resembling quicksand sucking you in continuously with vigorous motions.

At the start of your day, say a prayer of thanks for the food you eat, the clothes you wear, for being healthy and being able to move around freely; even moving to the other side of the room can be a simple pleasure. There are many other people around you, and in other countries, who are less fortunate and to have the bare essentials of a nice warm meal, or a nice warm bath and comfortable clothes that fit properly seem millions of miles away to some individuals.

Try also to find faith and understanding in God's teachings in the Bible, although there will be things in the Bible you don't understand. In the Bible it says, 'Seek and ye shall find'. This is the answer to all your questions, asking someone to explain to you about anything you do not understand, also praying to God for understanding of his words and their meaning.

Spiritual guidance at times can be quite soothing and comforting for some individuals; it can also be a turnaround to a new life of eyes opening and giving out an inner feeling of more peace and well-being for some people.

Mummy, I Won't Always Be a Child

'Mummy, what makes me an adult?' When you are eighteen years old, by the laws of society you are an adult. This means there are things you can do without parental consent. In other words, you do not have to ask permission if there is something you would like to do, for example, leave home, get married, learn to drive, vote, go into public bars to buy an adult drink.

In your heart and understanding of yourself, you must decide for yourself if you are responsible enough to make decisions in your life, and on your own, which will allow you to be happy and cautious, and enable you to live peacefully, without feeling sad, and always trust and believe in God to guide you.

The following are supportive suggestions for what's important in life:

• Believing in God, and having a conscience concerning what's right and what's wrong.

• Being happy with values and having respect for yourself and others.

• Taking pride in yourself in a healthy way. Keeping yourself neat and tidy and looking after yourself by what you eat.

• Enjoying life, trying new things and feeling a sense of achievement.

• Always listening and learning so you can strengthen your understanding about things.

- Sticking up for yourself; no one must boss you around.

- Good manners is grace. People will always mention that it is lovely to see Carla, she has such good manners.

The following are supportive suggestions for qualities that help a relationship:

- Trust and honesty

- Respect and good manners

- Kindness and caring

- A supportive friend, with whom you have similar interests you can enjoy together

All these qualities express the most important part in a relationship, which is communicating with each other, rather than talking at each other.

Thinking Positive

Thinking positive is to always keep trying at whatever you want to achieve.

Try to start your day with happy thoughts of, 'I am going to let the day take care of itself', expecting that at times you might feel happy and then suddenly there may be sad intervals, just when you least expect them, when all was going so well throughout the day. Out of the blue, uncertain changes give out feelings so distant from your aims and goals. Sometimes this can be all part of the trials on the road to success, just when you feel like quitting, hopeless feelings of echoes of continuous negative thoughts go through your mind. 'I cannot go on any more.' Sudden celebrations. An amazing turnaround. You cannot believe it. Triumph and victory, the opening of a new beginning for what you have always wanted to do.

Ambitions

Ambitions are strong desires to achieve something you have always wanted to do.

At times the journey to keep going for what you believe in, and for what you want to do with your life for the future, can seem so long and tiring, giving out feelings of uncertainty, resembling echoes of doubt whistling through the trees on a windy day, the constant howling so loud in tone, yet not being able to see what's ahead.

I always like to listen and, as I know and acknowledge, we can all learn things from each other. To keep going is my everyday thought and belief, but at times I have feelings of doubt.

Age, I have recognised, is a number only. An individual's advanced years does not make him or her more knowledgeable.

If you have not been taught something or have not taken the initiative, or have not had the opportunity to find out about something, are you experienced? Are you knowledge-able? Does age come into this matter? No, time and years may change and go up, but individuals young or old can broaden their horizons through communication from listening to each other.

Things do change, but more important is how you approach change for the better, hopefully with a positive step.

This can apply to both young or old being treated as individuals rather than according to their age.

Choices

Choices are about freedom of opinion, sometimes turning out for the better, or, unfortunately and unexpectedly for the worst.

We cannot predict that things will go well at any time, although coincidences can come about. You may have a good feeling about something you are going to try out, and it turns out to be the right thing to do, resulting in happy feelings of 'I was in the right place at the right time and this was meant to be.' When the choice you make doesn't go as well as expected, the suggested approach to have is to try to stay calm, by saying and believing that you did what you thought was best at that time, and learn to accept that things don't always go to plan.

Life is what you make it. It's a small word with a big meaning, full of challenges, changes, ups and down. There are triumph and disasters from life's experiences, as you wonder if you should or should have not, reflect on the past, present and future continuously.

The key is to look forward, rather than to look back, and say to yourself, and act upon it, that you did the best you could, at what you thought was right at that time.

Do not be too hard on yourself. Praise yourself for your achievements as you go along, accepting downfalls or disappointments if things do not turn out as expected.

You can learn from your mistakes as you go along; it's okay to get things wrong, because this is how we can learn to correct things, and deal with obstacles in our way. Shun feelings of rejection and thoughts of failure, negative shadows and echoes of endlessly ringing bells, chiming out,

'Why me?'

Tomorrow is another day, bringing at times smiles of joy and also, at sudden unexpected intervals throughout the day, rainfalls of tears.

Laughter

Having a sense of humour is very important. This means to be able to find a funny side to something someone has said or done and being able to respond by not taking it too seriously, even if it is not something you totally agree with your reaction is just to laugh.

A sense of humour is invaluable in a difficult or uncomfortable situation or environment. You can protect yourself from how you really feel about a group of people or even an individual person. When you laugh about something someone has said or done which you do not particularly like, most of the time you feel better for it. But there are some circumstances where you need to express yourself more directly in an assertive way, which means explaining to the individual that you do not like what was said or done, mentioning it in a meaningful way, so that they think twice before again saying something unpleasant indirectly or directly to you.

As you grow and learn about individuals, you will learn how to deal with people more confidently, and realise that some things are just not worth worrying about, and gradually a sense of humour and how to apply it will come about more naturally in your everyday approach to different situations. The more you do things the easier things will become.

Nature

Nature is to do with everything that God has created.

Nature paints its own picture always, which means that things take care of themselves, for example, the changing of the seasons. When it's spring the flowers bloom, providing beautiful colourful views all around in the gardens and in the parks. When it's summer you feel the warmth from the summer. When it's autumn the leaves fall from the trees. When it's winter the days grow colder and shorter, and the nights are longer.

Nature is reflected in people in that true beauty comes from the inside and is reflected on the outside. You do not need to enhance your outward appearance or put on an act for people to like you.

It's natural that there are some people whom we like more than others, and also with whom we get on better. Also there are occasions when some individuals just on sight alone let you know in their physical actions that they do not like you, without even taking time to get to know you first. This is quite silly really, but try not to take any notice, because they are not the only people on the earth, and there really isn't any point in going over it in your mind again and again, trying to work out why it is that this person dislikes you.

The suggested approach is to treat someone as you would like to be treated, with respect and also a kind and caring nature, and if you feel you are not being treated in this way, move on and find someone who will appreciate your qualities of being a nice person to be around.

Fashions

Looking after yourself regarding what you eat and how you think is very fashionable. The meaning of this phrase is that if you eat well most of the time you feel healthier physically in your daily activities, and also have more energy mentally in your everyday approach towards how you think and how you do things.

Another meaning of fashion, which is more recognisable, is what you wear and how you present the outfit. What you wear can make you feel more confident and socially acceptable with individual people or groups, but what really is important is feeling comfortable about what you are wearing, and not feeling that, if you do not wear the same style of clothes that everybody else is wearing, you are not going to look nice or fit in with the crowd, or no one will talk to you because you look so different.

Fashion is about you and your choice of clothes and style and whatever you feel suits you, regardless of whether you are smaller in size than someone else or bigger in size.

Being careful at times is necessary, so do be careful about the time and the place and the type of clothing you wear, because misunderstandings can often come about just by what you are wearing, and the outcome can be quite upsetting at times.

It is true that someone should not judge you by what you are wearing, but quite often, before someone gets to know you, they see what you are wearing and this is the first impression they will receive whilst getting to know you.

Responsibility

Responsibility means to take care of someone or something you have been asked to do by someone else. The role of being responsible is taking care of someone or several people. For example, a new girl, Stacy, has just started in my daughter's class at school, and her teacher, Sandy, has chosen Carla, my daughter, to sit next to her because she sees Carla as a friendly sociable girl and this will hopefully help Stacy to feel more relaxed on her first day, and hopefully help her to settle down more easily into the school's routine of daily activities in the classroom and around the school.

Another example of a responsible role is being a parent. This is a huge responsibility that involves being able to provide a loving stable home environment for your child to learn values and discipline concerning why we do or do not do certain things. Also children learn from parents as their first teachers through positive examples for growth and development for when they are adults, not forgetting that even adults make mistakes at times and do not know everything.

A mother's role is to have shared responsibility with the father for all the needs and care of the child and also to help with decisions and support, to enable the child to feel loved and cared for and secure whilst growing up into an adult.

A father's role is being responsible for his children, even if he is not living with their mother. His responsibility is to show an interest towards his children and give them support in their everyday needs and care, daily or spontaneously wherever he can.

Clear and honest communication at all times helps with children, although none of us are perfect. We all do the best we can.

Due to individual circumstances not every child has a mother and father at home, living together and sharing the responsibilities of bringing up their children.

Do not forget to find time to show an interest in your child's progress at school for parents' evenings encourage progress in areas where it is needed, and also give continuous support for how well they are doing at the moment in their present class.

At fun day events at school, like sports day or school plays, children really look forward to parental support and showing their parents how they are getting along. Also parental support boosts confidence and builds up their children's self-esteem.

General support in any decisions concerning the children's welfare of a second opinion is an instant absence to some individuals.

Quality is not to do with how much time you spend with children. Quality time with children is the method of approach you apply in communicating with children whilst you are around them, and the feeling all around between yourself and the children, resulting in personal satisfaction and feelings of well-being from growth and achievement in this time together.

Quality care with children is individual because, after all, we are all different; it is more to do with how you respond to questions that are asked by the children. Allowing children to express their opinion on something they are not sure about, although at times you feel exhausted. Patience is necessary for contentment around children, and also it is important how you feel about yourself and the development and progress of the stages your children are going through and how well you feel they are doing.

Sensitivity

Sometimes it can be so hard to walk away from something that someone said or did to you that was so hurtful and cruel. The angry feelings you have can be very unsettling to your mind so you endure mental torture as you talk to yourself and think, I should have said something. Why didn't I knock those words right out of their mouth? How dare they speak to me in that way? But at the time, my actions spoke louder than my words. I knew better, regardless of how it looked to other people, and their thoughts on how they would have handled the situation. I listened to my inner voice that was telling me to be stronger, because this would soon be only visions of yesterday.

Another example of sensitivity can be when you would like to give your opinion on a subject that is being talked about by a group of people, but you feel a bit nervous, because you do not want to stand out and feel like everyone is looking at you.

The suggested approach in dealing with this is to try and relax by listening carefully to what is being talked about, and then choose your words carefully, thinking about how you will express your feelings and views on the subject. Try not to worry if the words do not come out exactly as you would like them to; it happens to all of us at times, but remember there will always be another time, where it's not what you say, it's the way that you say it that counts.

Greed

Greed is having too much of something, sometimes knowingly and sometimes unknowingly. Sometimes you never know what you have got until it is gone.

Greed can come in numerous disguises, which means, for example, you are managing fine on a little money, but at times you have unbalanced and resentful thoughts and feelings, wondering how long things will be like this, and thinking that a little more money would make things much easier. In your conscious everyday thoughts, you go on mentally accepting and adjusting to the situation, telling yourself that things will not be like this for ever, only for a while, until you can see your way more clearly. Then all of a sudden unexpectedly, you are given more money as a gift. What do you do with it? In anxiety and craving and yearning, you spend all of the money, not intentionally, but with anxious unsettled feelings of 'I deserve it and I have been missing out on so many things I have been wanting for a long time, and now this is my comfort payment in return, to make me feel better about my situation.' Thoughts of spending half of the money and saving half for something that you really may need urgently resemble images of being in a desert all alone, miles from anywhere.

Reality has settled down again. All the money has gone. I am back to where I started. My unbalanced emotions of all my problems have not been solved, they are a continuous candle with flames flickering around me, giving out shadows of doubt, moving on and drawing strength from the weakness of lust, which means you are never satisfied with what you have got, and at times are envious and want to be like someone else. The continuous throbbing in your mind, echoing competitive thoughts of material gain from possessions is only temporary relief, and you display feelings of boredom at times, not knowing what you want to do, and appear never to have enough of anything.

Greed can be lonely without values, can be destructive and painful, and can also be blind to tones of misunderstanding of anger. It can also be unaware of resentful feelings of weakness and constant obstacles, from crying out with sadness at trying never to give up on the good things.

Try to hold on to support from your inner thoughts of doing the right thing, although at times difficult or awkward situations may lead you to be drawn in the opposite directions, leaving you with regretful feelings that can cause dark shadows to be constantly in your life.

Rage

Rage is to do with continuous anger. Sometimes, through unfair and unfortunate situations, you can be caught up in the middle between two people and a misunderstanding, or even a group of people. This can unfortunately result in being in the wrong place at the wrong time.

Sometimes rage can occur from within, resembling your mirror's reflection, from trapped feelings of insecurity or not knowing how to respond in a circumstance or situation, going over in your mind whose fault it really is. When reality speaks out, you cannot change anyone else but yourself, and in some situations it is best to just walk away and close the old doors and open the new doors to thinking positive. This means thinking straight with calming nurturing thoughts that better things are ahead, trying to put the past behind you, although you are not able to forget, but in time you will be able to move on and feel more relaxed about everything and yourself.

Sometimes, when you realise that individuals are unfortunately trying to hurt and upset you, when you have not done anything to them, the approach to take to protect yourself is to try to stay calm, and turn the tables on them. This means not to let them know you are upset by what they have said or done. Sometimes things have a way of taking care of themselves, although at this particular time it seems so unthinkable that this is the last possible thought in your mind, the way you feel at that moment.

To be able to control rage can be very hard, because it can arise at unexpected intervals, times and places. Yes, it is normal to be angry and to let out expressions of hurt and pain, as a release in dealing with a situation, but it is more important to be able to control a situation before it controls you, resulting in physical outbursts and mental torture or frustration. The way to approach this is not to let things get bottled up, which means do not ignore feelings of anger and disappointment, but be more assertive in being able to notice whether someone is cross with themselves for things not having worked out as expected and not with you and just be able to walk away and not take it personally, but deal with it professionally by ignoring it. After all, tomorrow is another day and some things are just not worth worrying about.

Rules

The purpose of having rules is to help and offer support with guidelines towards discipline, which means in certain situations how we behave and the reason why we behave in this way, and what we can gain from communicating in this way and by listening to each other.

Different parents set different rules. After all, we are all different and have different views on what we feel is best for our child or children. For example, some parents set bedtime at eight o'clock, whilst other parents set bedtime at nine o'clock. Rules are not about who is right and who is wrong. Rules are set by individuals.

Rules are meant for a quality of interest and care, for steering you in the right direction, for a better lifestyle and for the future. The rewards derive from developing your mind and thinking positively what you would like to achieve when you are an adult, and how to go about this, from a structure of care on a routine basis, providing you with love, care, stability and security, from people around you consistently showing you they care in their method of approach.

Prevention is better than cure, which means taking time out to think first before making responsible decisions which, hopefully, you will not regret later on, and also being able to make changes in your life for the better, and being able to accept and understand that it is normal when things do not always work out as expected. At times we all bend the rules, even adults.

Different tasks apply in different places and are meant for safety and security and to be carried out with the appropriate good behaviour, although misunderstandings can come about spontaneously from not thinking first why you have responded in an incorrect way, sometimes knowingly and some times unknowingly.

When we communicate with children about rules, we should talk with children, rather than at them. The difference is giving a child or children a say, to encourage them to express their opinion on something, when at times it can seem pointless, depending on the type of situation, whether it is good or bad.

Rules also help motivate and encourage patience and hope when you are trying to work towards taking time out to think first in how you approach and handle future situations.

It's not what you say and do that gets results; it is the way that you say and do something, encouraging realities from beneficial support only with communications to set you on the right track and actions to follow also.

Changes

Changes can be frightening, because when you are used to doing something always in a particular way that you are happy with, you see no reason for change.

Changes are all about learning and trying new things, broadening your horizons, doing things better, hopefully, the second time around, and also seeing your way clear with positive intentions for a brighter outlook and positive thinking about whatever your goals may be.

Changes are also about continuously developing your awareness, although they do not always turn out as you expect. Sometimes it can be hard to accept that this is all part of the learning process and that we will always be going through growing experiences and will just need to do the best we can in any situation we come up against, whether good or bad.

Trying to stay calm is a useful and beneficial approach to changes that will take place all around you, constantly and spontaneously.

Learning from your mistakes opens your eyes to positive changes, which means being able to reflect on where you went wrong, and think carefully about how you are going to do things better, and what approach you will need to take for drawing strengths from weakness, that is whatever gets you upset easily, whether it is a person, several people or a particular place where you don't like going. You will still be able to control the situation by your positive, determined approach, rather than let the situation control you, leaving you with feelings of frustration and anger.

Peace

Peace is a very personal and individual feeling of well-being, freedom and contentment in whatever the situation or circumstances may be.

For example, after a continuous phase of things not working out as you would have liked, causing you to feel unhappy, unsettled and worried in your everyday conscious thoughts, they are now only visions of yesterday, resembling a broken mirror's reflection. The problem that has been causing such torment to your mind has now resolved itself. This has come about by you letting the day take care of itself and being prepared to make your actions speak louder than your words.

When you leave your house in the morning or maybe even in the afternoon, try to think first about what is worth noticing, although at times you will be drawn unintentionally into a situation that may not always be for the better. Try to focus your thoughts and attentions only on your everyday travels to the shops or to school, noticing only happy surroundings that can help in starting your day on a relaxed feeling of well-being and looking forward to another day.

Treating others as you would like to be treated is a good quality to be able to express in your everyday movements, always remembering that individuals may not share the same views as yourself So try not to be upset by their difference of opinion and their actions, which may seem to you destructive and upsetting, yet draw observing crowds of people for attention and speculation.

The World

Taking an interest in your life. What would you like to do in the future? How do you go about achieving what you would like to do? Are you happy living in this country? Why not try another country and travel abroad?

It is a big world outside your front door. What is meant by this phrase is endless fun journeys and the challenges of travelling to different countries if you choose, taking the opportunity to find out about how other cultures live, from everyday conversations about what the is climate like, and what the atmosphere is to live in generally. Is it a small or large population? How do individuals live with each other and cope with everyday ups and downs on a daily basis? What's the traditional food like? Is it tasty with lots of variety of sweet and savoury flavours? Is the food expensive? What currency do they use? Are clothes expensive? What are the fashions like? Does it sound like a friendly environment to live in? Are there more opportunities in this other country than where I am living at the moment? Do I feel more respected and feel I am treated more equally and fairly by my colleagues, and also stand more chance of promotional prospects and moving forward at a more challenging pace for my future career?

Learning how to speak a different language can be very interesting and useful, giving you more flexibility in whatever career you choose. It is useful also for everyday communications professionally or socially, with people you meet on everyday travels and in being able to listen and understand and learn from each other, encouraging you to feel more confident and independent in your everyday interaction with different people from all walks of life, regardless of whether they are male or female, black or white, old or young, but just individual human beings like yourself with whom you could build relationships resulting in friendships from sharing similar interests.

Hobbies and Interests

Hobbies are things we take pleasure in doing in our spare time. Interests are things you enjoy taking time out to do. You learn about hobbies and interests from when you are a baby and a toddler without realising what they are called from your actions and reactions to playing with particular toys that give you hours of amusement because of how the toy sounds and feels, its attractive bright red and green colours and because it feels cuddly and warm. Every time you put it down, you always pick it up as your most appealing and interesting toy because it provides you with lots of fun and enjoyment.

As you get older and start to communicate, you respond in conversation mentioning that your favourite toy is Freddy, the teddy, and also mention that you like playing with Lego because you can make many imaginary things with it, and it comes in lots of interesting shapes and sizes and provides lots of fun whilst playing with it.

Children learn from the toys their parents or carers buy for them, which provide them with continuous entertainment for a while, until they are ready to go off and find another toy to interest them.

Reading is an excellent way to find out about what you are interested in and also for finding out about what things you would like to try and do.

Sports clubs or youth clubs are places of interest which provide many activities inside or outside for you to get involved in. They also help you decide what you like doing and they also provide opportunities for you to meet many other children of a similar age with whom you can make friends and have fun.

Having hobbies and interests also helps you to feel more confident and sociable around an individual or group of people; they also help when you have a conversation about what you have being doing, also about things you are looking forward to doing, and also provide you with opportunities and inspirations to try lots of different things.

Do not worry if you cannot find a particular interest or hobby that you like doing at the moment. In time you will know, but for now, keep on trying new activities and going to different places, and before you know it, you will have lots of hobbies and interests to keep you occupied, leaving you with happier feelings of contentment all round.

Children Learn From Adults

Our first teachers are the ones who look after us in the home environment. These people are usually our mother and father, although this is not the same for everyone. Children learn from their parents' actions and also their reactions, whether good or bad examples of right or wrong behaviour, sometimes knowingly and sometimes unknowingly, due to the misunderstanding of a situation or an occurrence and how it is interpreted.

When I am happy about something my daughter, Carla, has done well in, I praise her by mentioning to her how pleased I am with what I have seen and heard from her teacher at school, for example, very neat presentation in her handwriting book at school. This deserves a consistent reward because this is very important in encouraging an interest in what is written down and this also invites the reader to read more.

Sometimes I give Carla a choice of a gift she would like, with limitations on how much I can afford, so she understands that there are some things I can afford, and also there are other things I cannot afford because they are too expensive.

On other occasions, when I have been pleased with Carla at home for tidying up her bedroom after playing, I murmur words of encouragement in a friendly soft tone telling her how neat her bedroom looks. She smiles, her eyes sparkle brightly with delight, and then, in a soft voice, full of pleasure, she says, 'Thank you, Mummy.'

The message I am trying to put across here is that every time children do something well you do not always have to buy them gifts, because, like a tree, they grow from the seed from which they are sown.

When I am feeling annoyed about something Carla has said or done, the approach I try to take is to stay calm, enabling me to think first about what has actually occurred to bring about this anger, although in myself I am feeling tense, tired and frustrated, staying calm does help in trying to settle the matter. We do this by communicating with each other, rather than at each other. The approach I use is to listen to each other. First I listen to what Carla is explaining to me. Then I communicate with her, asking her if she is feeling a bit left out, or if she is deliberately responding in this way to get my attention about something someone has said or done, or is she just having a moment like I have myself at times, when you don't even know why you feel upset. Towards the end, Carla says she is sorry. I also mention that I am sorry, and if I have said something I should really not have said, I said it out of anger and because I felt a bit let down by her behaviour.

We shake hands and have a cuddle and ask each other if we are still friends. We both say yes, and then we carry on with the rest of the day, putting this situation behind us.

The message I am trying to put across is that, as crazy as it sounds, there is much more logic in trying to stay calm around anger, and trying to think first and talk things through, which is easier said than done, rather than just exploding, which does more harm than good, leaving you with more permanent mental and physical scars, which eventually result in flashbacks and not being able to let go of the past.

Temptations

Temptation is about persuasion and being able to lead an individual or several people astray.

At times we all get tempted into doing things that are not good for us, sometimes knowingly and sometimes unknowingly; this applies to adults and children.

Temptation can lie under the surface but in certain situations can slowly rise, in full bloom, to the surface.

Temptation can also be a sign of weakness in a person, who seems to find it hard to have values, although not always intentionally, and also they find it hard to be satisfied with what he or she has got, and believes that the grass is always greener on the other side.

To some individuals temptations are exciting mysteries that continuously provide thrills and daring adventures. To others temptations are constant nightmares and are often best forgotten because of their bad associations.

Temptations can be very competitive and glamorous to the outsider looking in, but reality unfolds and clearly explains that you should never judge a book by its cover.

Temptations can be moments of only temporary relief. Looking ahead, tomorrow can be a bright day, depending on what you choose and decide, what it is best to leave behind and how you approach the day, rather than the day take care of you with not always welcome responses.

Temptation is about learning how to say no to something or someone, and believing that you can really move forward and that actions speak louder than words, and being able to find an inner peace by taking control of how you communicate with others, and being able to stand up for yourself and individuals more assertively as far as what you would like to do for yourself, and what you also feel is best for you to say at any particular moment.

My daughter's favourite sweets are Starbursts, and one day I decided to buy her a packet of Starbursts for a treat. Normally I break off half of the Starbursts, trying to encourage her to save some for later, but on this occasion I decided to give her the whole packet. Carla was delighted. She munched and hummed and chewed, telling me how they tasted delicious and that she could not resist eating one after the other, because they looked so nice and tasted so yummy, and she just could not wait to get to the bottom of the packet to have a green Starburst, which was her favourite.

In age Carla is a child, but in understanding she is an individual. I approach her in a soft calm tone, asking her, 'Do you remember the other day when you asked me what temptation meant?' She responded and said, 'Yes, Mummy.'

I told her that she had just described temptation to me, without realising it, in her conversation about the Starbursts, and also in her actions of eating one after the other, and forgetting, although not meaning to, about saving half for after tea or for when we got home or for after school the next day.

Carla communicated with me saying, 'Mummy, I forgot,' and then wanted to give me back the last two Starbursts in the packet.

I gave her a reassuring cuddle on the bus, and mentioned that as there were only two left she might as well eat them. I did not want to make her feel that she had done something terribly wrong. I just wanted her to have an awareness and an understanding of what temptation meant through her own actions.

The next day after work, when I picked Carla up from

school, I decided again to buy her a packet of Starbursts. As usual we had a conversation about how the day had been. Carla said, 'Fine, Mummy. I will tell you more about today when we are at home.' I decide to give her the Starbursts and she looked up at me in surprise and said, 'I know,' and gave me half of the Starbursts and said, with a smiling face, 'Temptation! I will eat these after my tea.'

The message here is to be able to use actual situations to bring about understanding and awareness.

Time

Patience is a virtue, and good things do come to those who wait. Nothing ventured, nothing gained. The meaning of this sentence is that you should keep on trying no matter how exhausted you might feel at times. There is no time like today. This is the time, the place and the hour. Do not put off tomorrow if you can do it today.

Anything is possible through determination and will-power. 'Try' is a small word, but has a larger meaning, and can provide everlasting, rewarding and satisfying results from positive thinking, mind over matter and actions.

Giving someone your time is a priceless gift. What is meant by this phrase is that giving someone your time does not cost anything in money; it comes from a warm understanding within your heart, and a willingness to take time out to show someone you care and appreciate their efforts and consideration, or thinking of you always.

Time on the clock goes around continuously and waits for no one, and only stops when the batteries run out. Similarly your time is your own, so make the most of it before it is too late and time makes the most of you, causing you to feel sad, with hopeless regretful thoughts and visions of yesterday, and to wish you could turn back the clocks so that things could be different.

Boyfriends and Girlfriends

A boyfriend is a male friend or companion; a girlfriend is a female friend or companion.

When we like someone we meet for the first time, it is their physical appearance which attracts us. Then we start to have a conversation.

We are all different and have different tastes in the type of friends and relationships we choose. Getting to know someone takes time, because in the beginning, when we are getting to know someone, we only want to give a good positive impression of ourselves. Truly, most individuals communicate in this way at first. Then, when we have more experience in building relationships with different people, we do things depending on how our last relationship went, generally wanting to learn from our mistakes and feel stronger and more confident in ourselves, for the next time we try to get to know someone quite well.

Quite often individuals change once you've got to know them, so it can be quite useful to take things slowly before you feel this particular person is everything to you. Going out on dates, to the cinema or to parties or swimming with lots of different people is quite a good idea, because this helps you not to become too settled with one person too soon. Try to remember tomorrow is another day and you cannot know someone through going out with them once, although you may find you have lots of similar interests and hobbies in common, which you like to do together, and are already talking about planning a date for the next week to go somewhere else.

Remember there is one thing for certain and that is you

cannot know everything entirely about a person, but you can know in yourself what you like and what you do not like in an individual's behaviour towards you and you can do something about it. Remember also that you cannot change anyone but yourself. If things are not quite working out as expected, break free from that person sooner rather than later, because sometimes, when you stay with someone for the wrong reasons, this can often turn out to do you more harm than good, leaving you with unsure low feelings about yourself. It can affect your self-esteem and take away your confidence and the sense of being in control of your life and doing what you feel is best for yourself.

All relationships have their ups and downs, but when you find yourself with someone with whom you have more upsetting times than happy times, your actions should speak louder than words and you should move on, although at times emotional feelings can be very disturbing for you, causing you to feel very tired and confused, not able to think straight and feeling all mixed up about yourself and also the person that you thought would always be there for you in good times and bad.

Try to think positively and really believe in yourself, that you deserve better, and in time you will look back and see this as a passing affair, and realise that not every relationship you have will be like this.

Negative Thinking

Negative thinking is the opposite of positive thinking. It means you have no energy in your communications or actions in trying to do anything you want to achieve, and leaves you with constant drained thoughts of doubt and disbelief in yourself, feeling that nothing ever works out for you, resembling dark clouds in the sky with heavy rainfall, descending continuously, presenting a portrait of doom and gloom.

Negative thinking and feelings can come about as a reflection from your early childhood from feelings you had when you were a child, that you were never really wanted, which left you with inner, lost, resentful feelings towards yourself, everyone around you and anything you might like to do.

It is easier said than done not to put blame on a situation or a person, but what is important is to try and turn all the unhappiness around, by trying to make the best of whatever matter or situation or circumstance you may come up against, although understandably it depends on the type of matter, situation or circumstance. We are all individuals and we all have different weaknesses and for some of us it may take a lot longer to draw strength from a very low deep feeling that has been settled within ourselves for quite a long time, and also to be able to see a bright side to what has seemed like an endless stuck-in-the-mud situation, which feels like being sucked down lower and lower by quicksand and not being able to hold on to any support from any angle is very tragic and upsetting.

There is hope with negative thinking; turn it around to

positive thinking. The approach to take is to try and do this by truly believing in yourself and your capabilities and responding to your beliefs and ideas in a confident way. Try doing some soul-searching by learning to like and love yourself and writing down what your qualities are. These are things which you do well and enjoy doing. The more you write down and have conversations with yourself about what you have put down will eventually help you to recognise the steps to take to be able to approach anything or anyone you come up against in a more challenging and a greater feeling of well-being. Also you will see more clearly that you cannot change anyone but yourself, and will also be able to deal with things more easily and acceptingly.

The Difference Between Loving and Liking

To love means to have a warm liking to someone or something. To like means to find someone or something pleasant or satisfactory.

At times, although they are two different words, when we communicate in a conversation about how we feel about someone or something we can give the wrong impression, although not always intentionally. Just by expressing a great fondness for someone or something, a misunderstanding of what you are trying to say can come across as something else, leaving you with an awkward or an uncomfortable feeling about this person. Thinking carefully about what you say and the words you choose does help, although at times in some situations and with some individuals this can be easier said than done.

At times we all have difficulty, even as adults, in trying to express our feelings to someone we really care a lot about for being supportive, caring and trustworthy towards us, and how we really value this friendship and see this person as very likeable.

You can love things about someone, which can mean you really admire them as a person and find them very attractive in many different ways, and also get on very well with this person, have lots in common, and also have lots of fun and good times with him or her. At times it can feel like this is the only person in the world for you and that there will be no one else you could like as much. But be careful, because there could be someone else you feel about in exactly the same way as this person and then you could start to feel confused about what to do and what to say to him or her.

The message I am trying to put across here is at times try using your head, which means thinking things through thoroughly, rather than letting your heart take over in emotional confusion. Although I am not an expert myself, to be in love with someone and to have a strong liking for someone can be very different. If you are not certain about someone or something, take your time to get to know them quite well first of all.

Sometimes having a break from the person for a while can do you both some good, giving you both time to reflect on each other, and can also help in deciding from a clearer perspective if you will get back together in time. Some things take care of themselves without having to put too much effort into it, and also that some things are just not meant to be, although at that particular time thoughts of not being together or having to choose are far from your mind.

The suggested approach to take is to try to view this as the beginning of a friendship, or a friendship that was never meant to be.

Marriage and Families

Marriage is two people developing a friendship, then a relationship, and then the joining together of the two people, a man and woman, in a religious ceremony, quite often taking place in a church, or wherever they feel happy about getting married.

Individuals marry for different reasons. When you think about marrying someone, your intentions at the time are usually to stay with that person for the rest of your life through good times and bad times. This is not the same for everyone.

Some people have many years of friendship and love for each other, and continue in this way while in each other's company, while others find out sooner rather than later and not always intentionally that married life is not suitable for them.

Everyone has ups and downs in their marriage where things are just not working out between them and their partner, then after a good talk or even screaming at each other they are both back together again and are the best of friends.

Whilst you are married to someone this should be a happy time for you, growing together and learning from each other, also helping and supporting each other not only in times of need, but in everyday awareness, when you feel your partner will appreciate you being there and also vice versa.

A family is a set of parents and children all living as members in the same household. If you were born whilst your parents were together, either married to each other or whilst living together, this makes them your biological parents and means you were conceived in their relationship. If, after a while, your mother and father separate because things were not working out between them, and your mother and father marry again, the new husband or wife, by society's laws – which means the rules we go by in the world we live in today – become your stepdad or stepmum. This does not mean that you lose your biological dad or mum or that they do not love you any more or do not want to take care of you any more or take you out and have fun with you. It means you gain a dad or mum and now you have two of them, not always by choice but because of a situation.

Some children get on better with their stepparents than with their biological parents, and other children get on better with their biological parents. Some children like them both the same.

With families, like most things, it is better and easier for you to look at what you have got, and that's each other, rather than thinking about what you have not got and how things used to be, although, understandably, this can be easier said than done.

Secrets

A secret is very private and personal information you withhold from others.

Asking someone to keep a secret is all about being able to trust that someone. Being able to trust someone contributes to a very special role in friendships and also developing relationships. If an individual has chosen you as a friend in whom to confide their secret, they value you and see you as a trustworthy friend.

Treating someone as you would like to be treated is a positive approach to keeping a secret, and not telling anyone else, because you have been told in confidence, and also have been looked upon as a good friend to whom they can turn when times are bad.

If you betray someone's trust telling their secret to someone else either by accident or intentionally, to get back at someone for something they did to you that was not very nice, or because you could not resist the temptation to let the cat out of the bag, which means you disclose the secret.

No news is good news, they say. What you do not know will not hurt you, but sometimes things have a way of finding their way up to the surface. What is meant by this phrase is what goes around comes around, and if you do something you should not have done to someone else, things have a way of getting back at you just when you do not expect it, sometimes with devastating effects.

Intimate Relationships

An intimate relationship is a sexual relationship between two people, usually, but not always, a man and a woman. Having a sexual relationship is nothing to feel ashamed of. It is to do with the changes and feelings our bodies go through, girls developing into womanhood and boys into manhood. This type of relationship is usually kept very private and personal between both individuals.

Having sexual intercourse can be a very physical pleasurable experience usually between two adults involving close body contact and also the touching and caressing of different parts of each other's bodies. It is usually best between two mature adults who understand what is taking place between them and the feelings they arouse in each other. This is a natural act which usually takes place, and is best, when two individuals care a lot about each other, first of all having to know about each other slowly.

You should not feel pushed into having sexual intercourse; it should be through your own choice and not something you rush into whilst you are with someone of the opposite sex.

Television

Television can be fun, entertaining, exciting and good company for all of the family at times, and also for individuals who live alone, not only because of what's on the screen, but for some individuals the sound from the television is good company in the home.

We all have different choices about the sort of programmes that we like to watch and what we find interesting, whether it is a mystery adventure, a family film or series, a soap opera, a cartoon or a real-life film, or even the news to keep us informed about what's going on around where we live and also in other countries.

How much television children watch per day or week is usually decided by their parents or carers. As far as my daughter, Carla, who is six, is concerned, our daily routine during the week regarding the television is that when she gets home after school, she hangs up her school uniform and puts on the television whilst I am preparing tea. I allow her to watch television because it helped me with teaching her the time when she was nearly six years old.

How I taught Carla the time was by having regular conversations with her about her favourite programmes. Then we would sit down together and draw pictures of clocks to match up with the times her favourite programmes started during the week or at the weekend. For example, *Sister Sister* starts at 5 p.m. *Sabrina, the Teen Witch* starts at 4.15 p.m. *Clarissa* starts at 6.30 p.m. *Kenal and Kel* starts at 1.05 p.m. *The Rugrats* starts at 10.30 a.m. *The Simpsons* starts at 2.45 p.m. *Moesha* starts at 11.10 a.m.

Then we decided to make a poster with all her favourite

programmes on it and the times they started, and we put it up in our living room in our happy corner on the wall not far from the television

No matter how busy I was during the week or at the weekend, I would always make a conscious regular effort, whenever Carla wanted to watch one of her programmes, or even at times all of them – I would ask her first at what time the programme started. Then I would ask her where on the clock 4.15 p.m. was, and also whether it was the morning or the afternoon. Then Carla would put her pretend clock to that time and I would give her a big cuddle and say, 'Well done', and then I would allow her to watch her favourite programme and at the same time she was learning how to tell the time, and also finding it fun to tick or circle in the newspaper the times her favourite programmes started.

Some programmes are more suitable than others. We are all individuals and have different views on what we feel is suitable for our children to watch. Television can have a positive effect but also a negative effect. Supervision of what children watch is up to the individual adult, because at times a programme and what it portrays can have an upsetting effect, and not being able to understand can sometimes leave children with a very restless unsettled feeling, which can affect their everyday moods and way of thinking.

The Past

The past is what has gone by. It sometimes leaves you with happy memories of the way things used to be, and sometimes with empty thoughts which are like dark shadows and pitfalls of regret and heartache. Try learning from yesterday so you can make tomorrow a brighter, happier day to look forward to, although understanding that actions speak louder than words at times. Looking at quality rather than quantity in anything you choose to set out to achieve can help.

Breakfast is the first meal of the day; it not only gives you physical energy for everyday travel, but mental energy also to enable you to think first about why you should do something and also why you should not do something in connection with whatever you come up against throughout the day.

We can learn from our mistakes and make things much easier for ourselves through what we have learnt, and also grow stronger in our ways by developing our everyday awareness and ways of handling situations, unexpectedly or knowingly. When you cross the road you look left and right to see what's coming; the same applies to the past. Try to look forward and accept that everything happens for a reason, sometimes turning out for the better and sometimes unexpectedly for the worst. Try to focus your thoughts on whatever brings a smile to your face and leaves you with calm harmonious feelings of well-being and contentment, enabling you to think positively about what you have and also about your future actions.

The Present

The present is about now, and being able to recognise why every day is so valuable.

We all have thoughts about what we will be doing tomorrow or what we intend doing, but reality speaks out and confronts us, continuously warning us that we may never see tomorrow. Some individuals may see this as negative thinking and see you as a person full of doom and gloom in your conversations. Try not to get upset and remember that everyone is entitled to their opinion. We are all different and view things from a different outlook.

The present to me is about positive thinking, because you are living today and you can see what is good and bad around you. Also you have choices and opportunities in how you approach things and also in your way of thinking and using mind over matter in whatever you decide to do and how to go about it. This means not putting off things today for tomorrow, also prevention is better than cure in whatever situation or circumstance you come up against. My explanation of this phrase is to always value what you have and not what you do not have.

My health is my wealth and, without this, things could be much more difficult for me, and also I would be less happy. I give thanks for pleasures such as my eyes to see with and also having the choice to be blind to a situation if I choose to turn and look the other way; also for my nose to smell the fresh fragrance of flowers in full bloom; also for my ears to listen out for positive thinking and how to go about this, also for my mouth to be able to talk and explain my views on a subject or situation I am interested in learning about; also my arms which support my hands in everyday handling of things and picking things up and putting them down again; also for my legs to walk around or run around as I please.

I am lucky and I thank God for these wonderful treasures because I am aware that this is not the same for everyone.

If something is not working out as expected, whether it is a task you are trying to do or a relationship you are in with someone, try making some changes in yourself and the situation or circumstances, so you feel better about yourself – and do it today.

The message I am trying to put across is about being able to recognise opportunities now, and making the most of whatever you are doing, rather than putting off things for another day which you might never see.

The Future

The future is about looking forward rather than back at what could have been or what should have been and always wishing that you could turn back the clock to the past.

Looking ahead, dreams can come true through your efforts and determination to be strong-willed in your communications, in conversations and supporting actions, in whatever subject or circumstances or situation is put before you by choice, or even regarding a spontaneous matter or concern.

When facing constant challenges from lessons in life's experiences of ups and downs, try to keep your cool and feel positive about whatever you come up against, although this can be easier said than done.

Children at school should not feel pressurised into having an education, but should be made aware about how much easier things will be for them in the future and also about how much more interesting their life can be. They should be made aware of the value of choices and also how having an education behind them will make them feel more confident in making these choices. They should realise the flexibility of always doing or being what you want when they are a grown-up and also that, if things do not work out as expected, they can try travelling to a different country and see if they feel happier and also if there are more opportunities.

At times it is normal that things do not work out as expected or planned, but try not to give up because this is the key to the future. Try something else and try to look upon disappointments as learning experiences which everyone has, even adults. Sometimes, when you feel like giving up, remember that this is all part of the trials on the road to success, so try to stick with it, believing that better things are always ahead.

Food

The importance of food is to give our body energy to function mentally and physically.

Breakfast is the first and most important meal of the day, not only for children but also for adults, because when we awake in the morning our stomachs are usually empty and we need some food to give us strength and enable us to focus more clearly on the day ahead and whatever tasks or situations or circumstances we come up against. However, not everyone can eat first thing in the morning.

Every food you eat is good for you in different ways, although some foods are better than others, because they contain less sugar or less salt. For example, chocolate biscuits taste delicious but plain digestives are better because they contain less sugar. Frozen chips also taste delicious but, if you make your own chips by boiling the potatoes first in a pot of water and then bake them in the oven or fry them, they will contain only the salt that you put on after they are cooked.

Having food that is hot or cold is equally as good for you. For example, having a cheese and tomato omelette is just as good as a cheese and tomato sandwich; both meals have the same nourishing nutrients in their foods and contain proteins and vitamin C, which are good for our bodies and keep them well.

When preparing a meal what is most important is to consider the method of cooking, whether it is boiled, baked, fried, steamed or stewed. The method of cooking we choose can depend on many things, such as the budget, which means the amount of money parents or carers have to put towards buying the food each week and their lifestyle. This means how they live, whether they live together, if they have to work, or if they are single parents, with many other responsibilities at home to deal with and only a limited amount of time to do them.

Although it can be quite hectic at times, and also easier said than done, try encouraging children to help out with mealtimes, and suggest ways they can help in the kitchen. For example, they can put the pasta or the spaghetti in the pot. They can name five ingredients that are used to season the meat with and choose five fruits to make a fruit salad. They can take out the vegetables and salads from the fridge and lay the table for mealtimes. You can ask children for their suggestions about anything they would like to eat and ask them to make a shopping list of their favourite foods.

The suggested approach is to try and make mealtimes fun for the family and also yourself, although this can be easier said than done. Try to do this by encouraging children to try different foods and also to get used to trying lots of different tastes, because this will encourage more of a choice in what they eat.

School

Some children like school and adapt more easily to starting school and settling into the routine of the day's tasks and activities and quickly start to look forward to doing their favourite subjects set by the teacher. Others can take a little longer to feel relaxed and content in this structured routine and not being with or seeing Mum and Dad throughout the day for longer periods, and therefore the change can seem quite frightening, difficult and upsetting to cope with at first.

By law, every child has to start primary school between the ages of four and five and then, when they have finished their last year in primary school, they go on to secondary school. This is when a child is eleven years old, and they continue their education which means learning all about lots of different things, until the age of sixteen years. Then they can choose to leave school or choose to stay on and further their education. This means they continue at school more focused on what sort of job they would like to do when they leave school or go to college.

College is a centre of further education for both young people and adults and provides lots of variety and information about what type of work you would like to do when you leave college.

College offers you a change of environment in which to study whatever subject you are interested in. For example, my daughter, Carla, would like to be an English teacher when she grows up. She could do a course in learning how to be an English teacher.

Before Carla started school I regularly made a conscious

effort to familiarise her in everyday conversations about starting school so, when it was time for her to make the change from being at nursery and also from being at home with me, she was looking forward to starting.

We used to have conversations about how grown-up she would be when she started school, and also about how she would be meeting lots of different children, making lots of new friends and doing lots of interesting things. She would also have lots of stories read to her, and also read lots of interesting books, which would teach her about many different and interesting things. I also told her about how she would be doing lots of drawings and paintings and making things to do with what she would be learning.

The purpose of children going to school is for them to broaden their minds and ways of thinking by learning about lots of different things and also the teacher's method in explaining things to them. It also encourages independence in a child away from the home environment and around lots of other children.

The ways in which school supports and encourages children is in the more they learn about lots of different things, the more they are interested in learning and also feel more confident in themselves, their achievements, doing well and also in their everyday conversations with other children.

School is not a competition, and learning at school from your mistakes as you go along is all part of a natural process, and at times we all find some things easier to learn than others. A child should never feel forced into learning, or feel that, if they do not get things right all the time, they are not loved or cared for. The suggested approach to take, which can be easier said than done, is to think first about how you speak to children, because at times misunderstandings can come about because of how we are feeling about ourselves and the day can sometimes result in negative and unwelcome communication with the child.

Health

Health is all about how you look after yourself, and can be easier said than done.

As we grow up, we realise that some foods are better than others for us by how they make us feel physically. Some provide more energy than others.

We are all individuals and have different opinions about how we live and what we feel is the right way to look after ourselves, and what we choose to eat or not to eat. We differ also in what we think is best for us, the type of lifestyle we choose for ourselves, and also in the way we do things through our own choice or decision, which sometimes turn out for the better and sometimes unexpectedly, for the worse.

It is good to ask questions if you are not sure about something, rather than feeling because of your age you should really know the answer, and, thinking that you will be teased, refraining from answering. No, you should not feel this way; everyone has different circumstances.

Age is a number only and does not make you a knowledgeable person if you have not been given the opportunity, or have not been told how to do something.

Never feel ashamed of asking about something you are not sure about, because this knowledge might seem quite frightening at the beginning, but could benefit you and make you a happier person, sooner than you could ever have imagined, leading you on to a better life.

How I communicate with my daughter, Carla, about health is that I say to her, 'Try to look after yourself by treating others in the way you would like to be treated, and also to try to be kind and caring, although at times you may feel some individuals do not deserve to be treated in this way. Try to be calm rather than fly into a rage because some things are really not worth getting upset about, and sometimes it is best just to walk away from a situation or circumstance and look ahead. Most important,' I say to Carla, 'is to try to be proud of yourself for who you are on the inside and let it shine on the outside in a positive outlook.'

Books

The purpose of books is to broaden the reader's horizon, which means to give the reader lots of information on a choice of subject he or she is interested in reading about. We are all different and have different opinions and views on things that interest us, and also the type of books that we are interested in reading. For example, non-fiction means the subject that you are reading about is true and actually took place. Fiction is the opposite; the subject that you are reading about is imaginary, not true.

The knowledge that you can receive from books is greatly varied, which means that there is information provided for everyone, regardless of their sex, culture or religion.

Books come in all different sizes and topics of interest, which is useful if you want to carry the book around with you. Some books can be quite expensive depending on the type of book you are wanting to buy, for example, reference books and encyclopaedias.

Reference books and encyclopaedias are very useful books because they contain varied information not only about things in the country you are living in, but also about other countries, cultures and languages and most other subjects you are interested in finding out about. What is also useful is that you can use them at any library to obtain any information you might need.

Depending on what you like to read, books can be good company with many variations in subjects. For example, they can be funny, scary, exciting, amazing, sad, ridiculous, mysterious, factual. They can provide relaxation, companionship and even sometimes feel like a best friend.

When you read a book it cannot talk back, but it can be like a good friend in the advice, help and support that it provide. Books can guide some individuals just as a true friend would in deciding whether they should do something or not, and if they go ahead, depending on the situation or circumstance, what possible reactions they will get, back either positive or negative.

Books can describe a particular feeling you are going through, whether good or bad, and can be kept private between you and the book, until you feel up to confiding in someone else.

Breakfast, lunch, dinner, tea and snacks is also another way I would describe the useful purpose of books; the continuous energy you can get from the type of breakfast, lunch, dinner, tea and snacks you choose can also apply in the type of books you choose also.

The motivation you can get from reading and by wanting to keep on reading and also the inspiration from how something is put across can sometimes make you feel very relaxed and content.

Books can contain conversations in their chapters, also in different languages, which is very useful if you are travelling and going abroad or just want to learn another language or maybe even just as a hobby or an interest.

The message I am trying to put across in this chapter is have fun in your choice of books, enjoy what you are reading about and also make the most of the opportunities which books provide for learning about lots of different things.

Dreams

A dream is a series of pictures and events that go through your mind whilst you are asleep.

Individuals quite often dream about things that have been on their minds throughout the day, and in some ways they are trying to sort out a way in which to solve a problem arising from a circumstance or a situation.

Although it can be easier said than done at times, why worry? If things do not work out as expected, try to look at it as a learning experience and tell yourself it was never really meant to be.

Worry can cause you to feel restless or unsettled within yourself and can also blur your vision when trying to do something about a situation or circumstance. Try looking at your qualities and also things that you enjoy doing, and also things that you can do rather than what you cannot do. Always try to think positively and stay calm concerning a situation or a circumstance, although this can be very difficult at times.

When you dream, at times your mind travels in thoughts of wondering, hopes, desires and wishes for better things ahead. Dreams can come true. Anything is possible. This can often be to do with your strength and determinations to keep on working towards something you have always wanted to achieve, although at times the road to success can seem like miles away from nowhere.

Dreams can also be an awareness of an incident that is yet to surface, sometimes knowingly or sometimes unknowingly, and also sometimes your dreams can give out positive or negative warning guidelines to look out for when you wake up. This can be interpreted as prevention being better than cure.

Music

Music is to do with different types of sounds that can be made from playing different types of music, instruments and also from the type of music that is being played, for example, classical, hip hop, swing, jazz, gospel, pop, folk, blues, soul, reggae and melody.

We are all different and have different tastes in the type of music we like to listen to and also the feeling we get when the music is being played.

A positive aspect of music is its versatility which means that there is a lot of variety to choose from, regardless of age, colour, religion, culture and sex, and usually there is something for everyone to enjoy and listen to and also to dance to if they choose.

Individuals play music for a variety of reasons, because music can reflect the type of mood we are in, and our choice depends on how our day has been.

Music can also reflect a happy or sad mood, very deeply and descriptively, and also at times a very quiet mood or maybe even a dancing mood arousing exciting feelings of well-being. You could not wait until the end of the day to go home and put your music on.

For babies, the sound from a first toy, which can be a musical rattle, can bring about a smile of contentment and a wriggle from legs or arms, which you could interpret as a little dance. For toddlers, regularly hearing a particular nursery rhyme on the radio or hearing a nursery rhyme on a favourite children's television programme, can quite often encourage the child to sing and dance, leaving them with positive feelings and feeling more confident in themselves.

Music can also be used for celebration purposes, which means bringing lots of people together, regardless of age, sex, culture or religion, to enjoy and remember the happy day, for example, a wedding, a birthday or a graduation when an individual obtains a university degree. Celebrations can be a lot of fun and produce a relaxed, joyful mood in the crowds of people attending the celebration. People are usually smartly dressed, and usually they seem quite relaxed with other people and smiling.

The food is usually made up of lots of different kinds of foods, a buffet with party snack foods such as sausage rolls and sandwiches and many more, and also with lots of choice of hot and cold meals from different cultures and religions for everyone to enjoy.

The message in this chapter is that, no matter how busy you are throughout the day, although at times this can be easier said than done, try and always take time out for things that you enjoy doing.

Manners

Manners are to do with the way something is done and how people behave towards each other.

Having good manners is when you are kind and polite and also display good social behaviour, which means treating others as you would like to be treated, although some individuals do not always give the same respect in return. This can at times bring about a mixture of feelings regarding why some individuals, both children and adults, do not always behave in a correct way.

When children are well-mannered it makes the time spent with the adult who is taking care of them more relaxed and pleasant. On most occasions when the parents or carers arrive to take the children home the adults say how pleased they are about how well the children have behaved and that they would quite happily look after them another time. The children's mums, dads or carers are pleased with what they have heard and offer to buy their child or children a treat within a reasonable price range, which means nothing too expensive. The children are pleased with the response of their parents or carers, and also feel pleased with themselves and the treat of their choice they are going to receive because of their good behaviour.

It is much better to behave in the correct way with good manners, because, not only do people like having you around, you also feel much better in yourself and can also look forward to lots of treats, surprises, and visits to nice places. The message in this chapter is that, although it can be easier said than done at times, try to continue in the way you start, with good manners always.

Sharing

Sharing means to give an equal amount of something to an individual. Sharing and caring go together, because, if you care about someone or something, you show them in your actions, although at times, unfortunately, you may find you give more than you receive. Sharing is also to do with treating others as you would like to be treated yourself, although understanding this can be easier said than done, depending on the type of situation or circumstance and also how you are feeling at that particular time. For example, if a friend at school is upset about something someone has said and done, you will always be the first person to take time to show understanding for his or her situation or circumstance, but if it is the other way around, you may find that he or she is very distant and not so responsive and sympathetic towards you. Their non-caring reaction can at times make it more difficult for you to show sympathy towards someone else, if they are upset, although you may know or feel that what has happened is not their fault.

In talks I have with my daughter, Carla, who is six years old, I advise her to try to always be in control when it comes to individuals' responses, whether kind or unkind, knowingly or unknowingly. They respond without thinking first and only consider themselves.

We all have good days and bad days and, if an individual is friendly today and not so friendly the next, try not to get upset by this, because although it can seem unfair and not nice, we are individuals and have different ways of handling a situation and ourselves. We are not always able to respond calmly or walk away from a situation or circumstance knowing that we will feel more relaxed and content when the next day comes around.

The message I am trying to put across in this chapter is to try to take each day as it comes with sudden changes in individuals' attitudes and moods, which can always be just around the corner when you least expect it.

Chores

Chores are routine tasks that encourage you to take pride in yourself and also in how you look after things around you. The purpose of having chores is to encourage discipline and responsibility through the reasons why we do things and the way in which we do particular things and also what we can learn from this.

Parents and carers encourage children around the home to do everyday routine chores, such as keeping their bedroom tidy, folding up their clothes when they put them away, hanging up their school uniform on a coathanger when they come in from school, and also tidying up their toys after they have finished playing. To the child this can seem like a lot of the time Mum, Dad or the carers are nagging and fussing too much.

What you learn from doing chores is to be aware of your own health and hygiene and of how others will treat you, if they find out you have been taught respect and are responding to this approach in the way you communicate and the things you say and do whilst you are around others.

Regarding my daughter, Carla, I tell her regularly that the quicker she does her chores the more time we shall have to play games together and also the more time she will have to also play with her toys. I also tell her that I have my routine chores which I do everyday to encourage personal hygiene, in caring for her, and also in keeping the house clean. I also consider what I say and how I do things around others and also how individuals treat me, depending on how I communicate with them.

I often mention to Carla that it is not a person's age that

makes him or her an adult, it is how he or she copes with responsibilities and decisions, for the better or for the worse. Age is a number only, although by law permits you at eighteen years old to buy an adult drink in a public bar, or leave home without having to have your parents' permission. You also have the right to vote.

The message I am trying to put across in this chapter is that carrying out chores does you more good than harm, and also can help direct you in the correct pathway to becoming an adult.

Pocket Money

Pocket money is usually given to a child or children to help encourage independence in the handling of their own money, and also for them to spend it on things they like.

The amount of money a child is given each week or at the weekend usually depends on the family budget, which means how much money parents and carers can afford to give the child after putting money towards the household expenses each week or month, for example, food shopping, cleaning, equipment, bills, clothes.

In some situations not all children have two parents who are living together at home who help and support each other in sharing the responsibilities in buying the household items that are needed each week and providing pocket money each week or at the weekend for their children. For a one-parent family, only one lives at home either parent, Mum or Dad, it can be a tremendously difficult responsibility to try to manage a budget on only one income. This means money coming from one parent only has to be enough for all the family each week, and this can cause frequent upsetting misunderstandings amongst the children.

All parents differ in their views and opinions on how much money they consider enough for their children each week or at the weekend. For example, some parents give larger amounts whilst some parents give smaller amounts.

For children, having regular money at first can be fun and exciting and their instant thoughts can be that they just cannot wait to spend it all at once, sometimes on something they really have always wanted to have, or sometimes on something that someone else has always wanted to have, just to feel they will fit in with their friends and have something to talk about when they meet up at school or at the weekend. This way of thinking is quite normal and for some children it can take a little longer to be more assertive and disciplined in how they handle their own money. It can help to look upon this as a growing experience and realise that things will not always be like this for ever. As an adult, on some occasions you can recall your own first experiences as a child in handling money, which were not always the best at times.

The message I am trying to put across in this chapter is that it is not the amount of money you have, it is how you manage it.

Play

The word 'play' means to occupy yourself in something you enjoy doing, for example, a game or an activity like swimming. We are all different and enjoy playing in different ways or doing different activities to occupy our time and amuse ourselves.

The type of toys or activities, which parents and carers buy for children, help with the learning process in play, and also encourage children to be more aware of the things we do around us, and also the things we should not do, and also the reasons why we should not do them.

The purpose and importance of play for children is that it encourages learning in a relaxed way, not only by the type of toys you buy for your children but also in how you personally interact with them, also your method of approach in how you put across ideas and suggestions for play. These result in a happy, enjoyable, learning fun time whilst you play with your children, but also in a feeling of well-being and contentment for yourself.

Quality playtime means the way in which you play with children, for example, in a fun interesting way for the child and also for yourself. Quality time with children is more important and beneficial for them and also yourself, because it results in a good feeling for both of you, and this encourages you both to look forward to another occasion of fun and learning while you play.

Quality play can also mean the length of time you play with a child, which can only be useful if your method of approach continues in the way it starts. This can be very difficult at times, because children can become distracted and feel bored very easily, and for adults this can become quite tiresome and off-putting, and for children sometimes this can discourage the fun-time learning process.

The message I am trying to put across in this chapter, not only for children but for adults also, is that it is not what you do sometimes, it is the way that you do it that can produce positive results.

Grandparents

Our grandparents are the parents of our mother and father. Our grandparents can also be regarded as senior members of our family because they are the eldest.

From our grandparents, we can learn about lots of things that happened in the past, to do with history, which means events that happened a long time ago before we were born.

The way in which our grandparents talk to us can be very comforting, because they usually sound so relaxed and interesting in the way they explain anything to us, and also they are usually to happy with answering lots of questions about the way things used to be when they were children and also general questions that we choose to ask them. For example we can ask them, 'What was school like? What places did you like to go to, and also why was this your favourite place? What type of clothes did you used to wear? What was your favourite television programme? What did you want to do when you were grown up? What was your favourite country you visited? What were the sweets like a long time ago? What was your favourite food?'

What's nice about having grandparents is that, if they live with you, you have more members of the family to talk to. If Mum or Dad are busy with housework or if they are at work, there is always someone there whose advice you can always ask about homework or about a friend at school. If your grandparents do not live with you, this can also give you an opportunity to spend the weekend with them and also talk about all the things you have been doing at school, and also any nice places that you will be visiting soon and how you are looking forward to going.

Unfortunately not every child has grandparents to whom they are able to talk on the phone or go to see; this is not always through choice but because of the situation.

The message I am trying to put across in this chapter is: sometimes you never know what you have got until it is gone. So always try, no matter how hard it may seem at times, to look on the bright side.

Names

Our name is what we are known by and what we are called. This is the most important part of our self-identification. For example, my daughter's name is Carla Duval.

As babies we are given the names chosen for us by our parents. The purpose of us having a name is not only for individuals to know what to call us, but it also is a polite way of greeting someone and also getting to know them.

Some children are content with their names, whilst others would prefer to have a different name. Some individuals make themselves feel better by asking their friends to call them by a different name, and this makes them feel better about themselves and their social contact with others, when their friends do as they ask. When you become of age, at eighteen years old, by law you can change your name without having to have your parents' permission first of all. You can go along to your nearest registry office, which deals with enquiries about births, deaths and marriages, and they will be able to give you advice on how to go about changing your name.

As you go about throughout the day, everything you pick up has a label or a name of some kind on it. For example, when you read the title of a book, you may immediately think that it is something you would not like to read, but then you quickly turn over to the first page and read what is on it you then you change your mind, because it seems interesting and is the type of book to which you can relate and get useful ideas and suggestions from. Another example is that someone's name may sound strange and peculiar on the telephone, but when you actually meet up with that person, you may find out that this is a very nice friendly person and that is has been a very pleasant interesting occasion and you are looking forward to meeting up with this person again.

The message I am trying to put across in this chapter is to try to always look further than the title or the name of someone or something, because it is always what is on the inside of a person that counts.

Having Faith

To have faith means to have a strong belief in someone or something. Try always to have faith in your hopes and desires and believe that anything is possible if you are strong-willed and determined, although at times you will feel tired, weary and restless and feel like giving up. We can learn a lot from listening to each other, because this is the way we get to know each other and build relationships.

Learning is never a competition about who is the best or who gets their work right all the time. Learning is about taking an interest in what you have been taught, and more important, being able to understand the meaning of what is being explained to you, and if you do not, asking the teacher to explain it to you again.

What matters is not the child who reads the book first in class, it is that the child that understands what he/she has read, and if he or she is asked by the teacher to explain what the book is about, he or she is able to do this. Also what is important is not the child in class who finishes his or her work first, it is the child who presents his or her work well, and who also understands what he or she has written down and also understands the meaning of the work he or she has completed.

It is not what you do that counts, it is the way in which you do something and your method of approach, which usually gives you positive pleasing results in return.

We are all individuals and we can grow and learn from each other in sharing our opinions, experiences of good and bad times and the meaning of values in doing things and being able to recognise what we can achieve from our own efforts in anything we set out to do.

A calm approach, although this can be easier said than done at times, depending on the type of situation or circumstances, can help you to think first about how you can deal with responses, which, either intentionally or unknowingly, are not very friendly.

The message I am trying to put across in this final chapter is that having faith is a positive outlook on anything that you come up against.